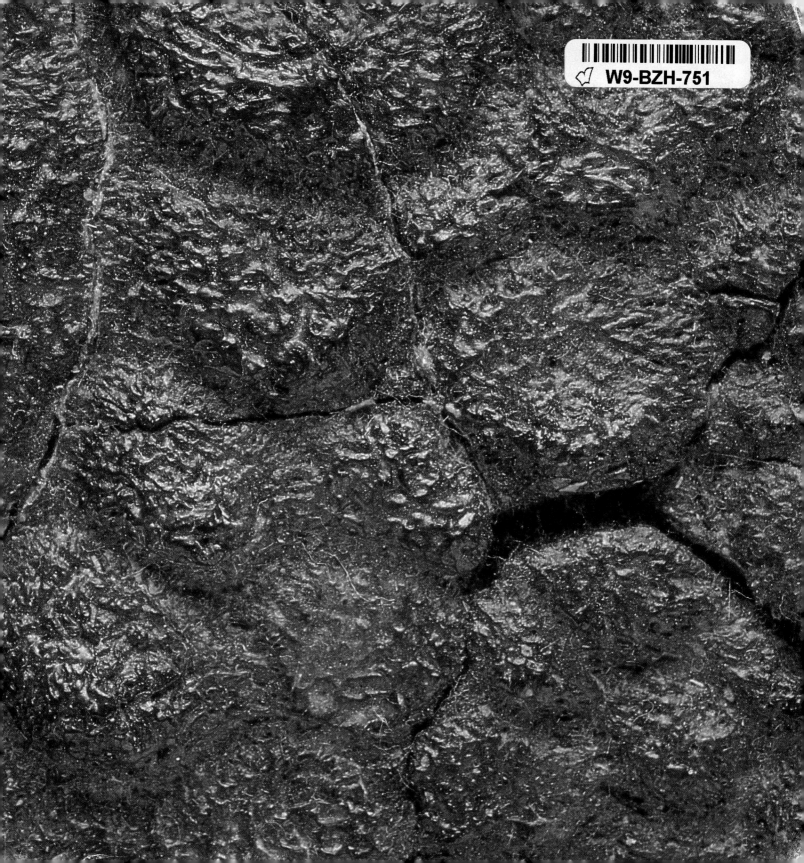

giang

prehistoric life
explained

A Beginner's Guide to the World of Dinosaurs

JINNY JOHNSON

Consultant: Professor Barry Cox

A Henry Holt Reference Book
Henry Holt and Company
New York

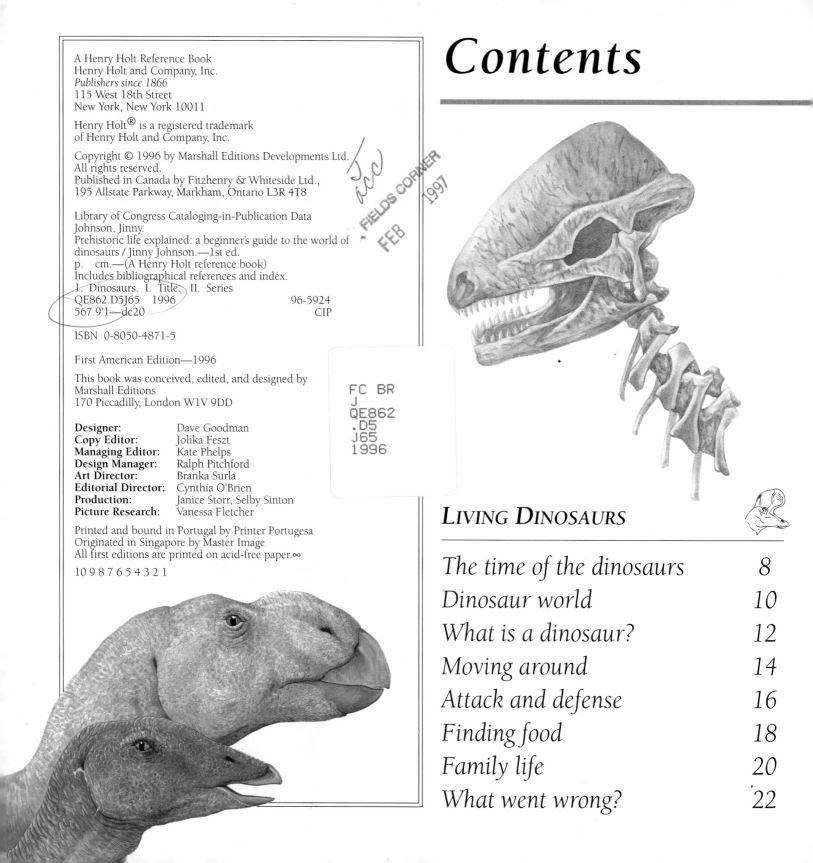

A Henry Holt Reference Book
Henry Holt and Company, Inc.
Publishers since 1866
115 West 18th Street
New York, New York 10011

Henry Holt® is a registered trademark
of Henry Holt and Company, Inc.

Library of Congress Cataloging-in-Publication Data
Johnson, Jinny.
Prehistoric life explained: a beginner's guide to the world of
dinosaurs / Jinny Johnson.—1st ed.
p.   cm.—(A Henry Holt reference book)
Includes bibliographical references and index.
1. Dinosaurs. I. Title. II. Series
QE862.D5J65   1996   96-5924
567.9`1—dc20   CIP

ISBN 0-8050-4871-5

First American Edition—1996

This book was conceived, edited, and designed by
Marshall Editions
170 Piccadilly, London W1V 9DD

Designer: Dave Goodman
Copy Editor: Jolika Feszt
Managing Editor: Kate Phelps
Design Manager: Ralph Pitchford
Art Director: Branka Surla
Editorial Director: Cynthia O'Brien
Production: Janice Storr, Selby Sinton
Picture Research: Vanessa Fletcher

Printed and bound in Portugal by Printer Portugesa
Originated in Singapore by Master Image
All first editions are printed on acid-free paper.∞

10 9 8 7 6 5 4 3 2 1

Contents

LIVING DINOSAURS

LIVING DINOSAURS

DINOSAURS WERE PERHAPS THE MOST SUCCESSFUL ANIMALS THAT HAVE EVER lived. These amazing reptiles ruled the planet for about 140 million years. They were masters of the land, but winged reptiles called pterosaurs flew in the skies while ichthyosaurs and plesiosaurs dominated the oceans.

The time of the dinosaurs

These creatures first appeared about 225 million years ago, during the period of time known as the Triassic. They became much more diverse and numerous in the Jurassic and only died out at the end of the next period, the Cretaceous. Even though they lived so long ago, dinosaurs were much closer in time to us than they were to the beginnings of the world. The Earth itself formed out of a mass of dust circling the Sun about 4.5 billion years ago. Imagine this vast length of time is like a race track 100 yards long. Dinosaurs evolved only five yards from the finishing line, and human beings appeared only a few inches from the end of the track.

◀ **Sharp-beaked Protoceratops** defends its eggs against a predator.

CENOZOIC
65 to 1.64 million years ago

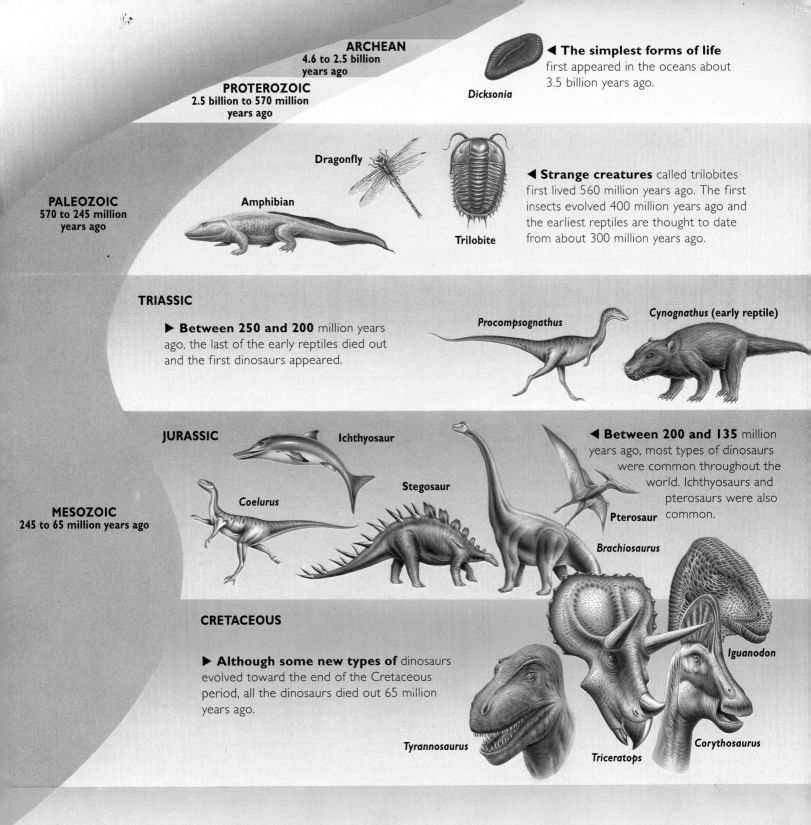

ARCHEAN
4.6 to 2.5 billion
years ago

◄ **The simplest forms of life**
first appeared in the oceans about
3.5 billion years ago.

Dicksonia

PROTEROZOIC
2.5 billion to 570 million
years ago

PALEOZOIC
570 to 245 million
years ago

Dragonfly

Amphibian

◄ **Strange creatures** called trilobites
first lived 560 million years ago. The first
insects evolved 400 million years ago and
the earliest reptiles are thought to date
from about 300 million years ago.

Trilobite

TRIASSIC

► **Between 250 and 200** million years
ago, the last of the early reptiles died out
and the first dinosaurs appeared.

Procompsognathus

Cynognathus (early reptile)

JURASSIC

Ichthyosaur

Coelurus

Stegosaur

◄ **Between 200 and 135** million
years ago, most types of dinosaurs
were common throughout the
world. Ichthyosaurs and
pterosaurs were also
common.

Pterosaur

MESOZOIC
245 to 65 million years ago

Brachiosaurus

CRETACEOUS

► **Although some new types of** dinosaurs
evolved toward the end of the Cretaceous
period, all the dinosaurs died out 65 million
years ago.

Iguanodon

Tyrannosaurus

Triceratops

Corythosaurus

Dinosaur world

▲ The ginkgo, or maidenhair tree, is the last survivor of a group that was common in the time of the dinosaurs.

Our planet may seem solid, but in fact the continental landmasses are continually moving around on the Earth's surface. This movement is slow—about the same as the rate at which your fingernails grow. But over long stretches of geological time, continents can move great distances and can also break up into fragments and join together in new patterns.

Not only were the landmasses different when the dinosaurs lived, but there were also no icecaps near the North and South poles. So warmer climates reached much farther toward the poles than they do today, and animals and plants were able to live all over the landmasses.

▼ CRETACEOUS
North America drifted farther from Europe and seas divided North America, Eurasia, and Africa.

▲ TRIASSIC
All the land was joined in one enormous continent, now known as Pangea.

Deep oceans are shown in dark blue and shallow seas covering parts of continents are light blue. Dotted lines show where the great single continent broke up to form the continents of today.

▲ JURASSIC
Pangea started to break up into separate continents. Shallow seas spread across parts of the land, dividing it even more.

◀ **In this Jurassic landscape** are many plants with fernlike leaves. Some of these grew as tall as small trees and some had seeds like those of flowering plants. The most unusual were the cycads with their stubby trunks.

▼ **During the Cretaceous** period the first flowering plants evolved. They may have looked similar to the magnolia flowers of today and were the first plants to have bright petals and perfumes to attract pollinating insects.

The spread of plants

Because there was only one landmass during the Triassic, the first dinosaurs were able to spread all over the world. But great areas of this land were very far from the sea and were extremely dry. During the Jurassic period, seas spread across parts of the land, and the climate became wetter and less hot. Many new types of conifer tree evolved, such as the monkey puzzle tree. Other larger plants included maidenhair trees, tree ferns, and cycads. Smaller plants included some with fernlike leaves which bore seeds instead of tiny spores like true ferns.

Plants with flowers which attracted pollinating insects did not evolve until the early part of the Cretaceous period, about 120 million years ago, and did not become common until later in the Cretaceous, about 95 million years ago. They first appeared in the warmer lands near the equator and then spread northward and southward until they were found all over the world. With such competition, cycads, ferns, and horsetails, so common in Jurassic times, became increasingly rare.

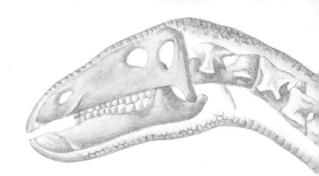

What is a dinosaur?

Dinosaurs were reptiles. They had skeletons like those of reptiles today, and impressions of the skin of some mummified dinosaurs show that they had the same leathery skin. This protected them from losing moisture through the surface of the body and drying up in the sun.

Living reptiles lay eggs with a leathery or hard shell, as do birds, which are descended from dinosaurs. Dinosaurs, too, are known to have laid eggs—some fossil eggs have been found with tiny dinosaurs inside them. All dinosaurs lived on land. Other reptiles, such as plesiosaurs, swam in the seas, and pterosaurs, flying reptiles with leathery wings, filled the skies. But no dinosaur ever swam or flew. All dinosaurs are now extinct. They died out 65 million years ago.

▲ Triceratops had the horny beak typical of ornithischian dinosaurs.

REPTILE EGGS

Amphibian eggs are jelly coated and have to be laid in water. A baby reptile is much better protected by its hard- or leathery-shelled egg. It can develop inside the shell until it is ready to hatch out as a miniature reptile, able to live independently on land.

Reptile egg

Amphibian egg

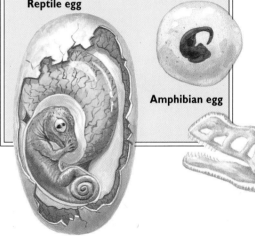

Two groups of dinosaurs

Dinosaurs can be divided into two groups, which differ in the structure of their hip bones—the saurischians and ornithischians. Both groups included several different families of dinosaurs (*see pages 36–37*).

In the saurischian dinosaurs, the three bones of the pelvis only connect with one another near the hip joint, where the hind leg meets the hip. In the ornithischian dinosaurs, two of the three hip bones also run parallel with one another downward and backward, away from the hip joint.

In both groups, there were some dinosaurs that walked on two legs and others that walked on all fours. The saurischians, though, were more varied in their lifestyles than the ornithischians and included fierce, flesh-eating predators as well as plant eaters. All the ornithischians fed on plants. They had an extra set of toothless bones at the front of the skull which were covered by a beak made of horn for cropping leaves.

Both groups included little dinosaurs that were less than 3 feet long. But the largest saurischian dinosaurs, the sauropods, were enormous—at least 98 feet long—while the biggest ornithischians, the duckbilled dinosaurs, were only 42 feet long and more lightly built.

Pubis

Ischium

Ischium

Pubis

▲ *Ornitholestes*
was a saurischian dinosaur
with a pubis bone pointing away
from the ischium bone. About 55
percent of dinosaurs were
saurischians, including
the great sauropods and
carnosaurs such as *Tyrannosaurus*.

▲ *Iguanodon* was an ornithischian
dinosaur with a pubis bone running
below the ischium bone.
About 45 percent of
dinosaurs were ornithischians,
including stegosaurs, duckbilled
dinosaurs, and horned dinosaurs.

Moving around

One of the secrets of the dinosaurs' success was that they evolved a better way of moving than other reptiles. Most early reptiles moved like lizards do today, with their legs sprawled out sideways. Dinosaurs held their legs straight down underneath the body. This meant their legs could carry more weight, and dinosaurs could become bigger and heavier. And they had only to lengthen their straight limbs to be able to take longer strides and so move farther and faster. The proportions of a dinosaur's legs depended on its size and whether it moved on four legs or two.

◀ **Sharp-clawed toes** helped *Diplodocus* to keep its footing.

A balancing tail

Whether 90 feet long or only the size of a chicken, all dinosaurs had long tails. Many used the tail to help them balance the weight of the front part of the body, allowing them to run on their hind legs. Some dinosaurs, such as *Gallimimus*, evolved very long hind limbs so they could run fast when hunting prey. Their legs had long thigh and calf bones, with big muscles in the thigh that pulled the leg back, driving the body forward. The bones of the ankle were also long and, together with the bones of the foot, acted as the final part of the lever that pushed the dinosaur along.

Many of the two-legged dinosaurs had extremely small front limbs, useful only for grasping prey and

A NEW WAY OF MOVING

Lizards move with a sprawling action, twisting the body from side to side with each step. The stance of the dinosaurs was very different. With the legs held underneath the body, dinosaurs could move with long, rapid strides, swinging the limb from the shoulder or hip.

Dinosaur

Lizard

▶ **Small, two-legged** dinosaurs had long slender limbs and light slim feet. The legs of a plant-eating giant were very different. The ankle bones were much shorter and the foot spread out to form a large pad to support the creature's weight.

handling food. The arms of the mighty hunter *Tyrannosaurus* were so small they did not even reach up to its mouth.

Mighty plant eaters

Some plant-eating dinosaurs, such as *Iguanodon*, could rear up on their hind legs when they wanted to move quickly or reach food. But they would drop down to all fours when moving more slowly or when feeding. Their legs were large and bulky, and some of the fingers ended in little hoofs.

The biggest dinosaurs, giant herbivores such as *Camarasaurus*, had bodies so large that they had to support their weight on all four legs. They could not move on two. The body had to be huge to allow room for vast amounts of plant food while it was slowly digested.

▶ **Gallimimus** could probably sprint at up to 40 miles an hour. Herds of these birdlike dinosaurs sped across open plains searching for prey. Speed was also their best defense against danger. They did not have sharp teeth or big claws to protect themselves from attackers.

◀ **Sauropod dinosaurs** such as *Camarasaurus* plodded along on thick pillarlike legs. They relied on their bulk to protect them from attack.

Long slender ankle bones

Slim three-toed foot

Short thick ankle bones

Heavy five-toed foot

15

Attack and defense

Life and death struggles went on between dinosaurs just as they do between animals today. Predatory dinosaurs attacked others for food. Plant eaters defended themselves against the meat eaters—and sometimes against rivals of their own kind. Sheer bulk was the main defense of the largest dinosaurs such as *Diplodocus* and other sauropods (*see pages 38–39*). Sauropods could also have used their long tails to defend themselves. Marks on the tail bones of *Diplodocus* show that large muscles powered the tail, allowing the dinosaur to lash its whiplike end from side to side to fend off enemies. If a sauropod reared up on its hind legs, it could also have used the claws on its front feet as weapons against attackers.

◄ **A tyrannosaur** attacked by making a sudden dash toward prey, then killing it with a bite to the neck.

▲ **Dromaeosaurs** also had an extra-large claw on each back foot which they used to slash at the flesh of prey.

16

Weapons and armor

Other large dinosaurs such as the duckbills (*see pages 48–49*) found safety in numbers. They traveled in herds, keeping the young and more vulnerable in the middle of the herd. Smaller dinosaurs relied on speed to escape from danger. Ornithomimids, for example, could make high-speed sprints away from enemies.

Many kinds of dinosaurs had built-in protection against enemies. Horned dinosaurs had a fearsome array of horns and spikes on their heads. They may even have gone on the attack when threatened and charged the enemy with their horns. Stegosaurs had bony spikes on their tails, and some armored dinosaurs (*see pages 54–55*) could defend themselves with the bony club at the end of their tails. Armored dinosaurs and stegosaurs were further protected by the plates of bone which covered much of their bodies.

▶ **With the massive horned head** held low, horned dinosaurs such as *Styracosaurus* warned off their enemies.

Speed was also important to an attacking dinosaur. Smaller hunters, particularly, relied on being able to make high-speed chases after their victims before seizing them in their sharp claws. Predators, such as dromaeosaurs, hunted in packs just like hunting dogs do today. Together they could bring down prey much larger than themselves.

The largest hunters, such as tyrannosaurs, were built for power and strength. They had massive jaws and daggerlike teeth which they could use to kill and rip apart prey in seconds.

▲ **The tail** of a stegosaur was armed with sharp spikes. This could be swung against an attacker.

Finding food

Like animals today, dinosaurs would have spent much of their time finding enough food to eat. Plant eaters have to search for suitable plants and eat large quantities of them every day in order to get enough nourishment. Hunters have to track down and catch their prey, but one good catch may satisfy them for several days. Some flesh-eating dinosaurs were small, but they could hunt larger prey in packs. Others, such as the tyrannosaurs, were large, heavily built creatures with powerful jaws and teeth.

There were many more plant-eating dinosaurs than flesh eaters. But they would have avoided competing with one another by feeding on different plants and at different levels.

Hadrosaur

PLANT EATERS AND HUNTERS

Duckbilled dinosaur Edmontosaurus was a plant eater. It chopped mouthfuls of leaves with the toothless beak at the front of its jaws. Farther back, banks of tightly packed teeth formed a grinding surface to break the food down.

A meat eater, Allosaurus had powerful jaws lined with about 60 sharp fangs. The teeth curved backward and had serrated edges like steak knives for slicing into the flesh of the prey.

Sharing resources

The smallest plant eaters would have grazed at ground level. *Protoceratops*, for example, had powerful jaws and strong teeth that could chop up the toughest of plants. Larger horned dinosaurs could have fed on low bushes, but had short necks and could not stretch up far. This type of dinosaur had a sharp, toothless beak which it used to bite off mouthfuls of plants. The food was then chewed with the grinding teeth farther back in the jaws.

Hadrosaurs were bigger than elephants today, so must have needed to eat a huge amount of plant food. These dinosaurs probably reared up on their hind legs to reach leaves higher up on the trees. Biggest of all the plant eaters were the mighty sauropods (*see pages 38–39*), which could stretch up to the fresh growth at the tops of trees that no other creatures could reach. They had long, slender teeth that grew only at the front of the jaws.

Sauropod

▼ **A group of plant-eating dinosaurs,** ranging from little *Protoceratops* to a giant sauropod, feed peacefully together, each at its own level.

Horned dinosaur

Protoceratops

Family life

As far as is known, all dinosaurs laid eggs, like most reptiles today. It was once thought that dinosaurs simply buried their eggs in a pit in the ground and left them to take their chances. But discoveries of duckbilled dinosaur nests in Montana and in Asia have shown that some dinosaurs at least guarded and cared for their young.

The Montana find seems to be the remains of a nursery of 75 million years ago, where duckbilled dinosaurs laid their eggs and young developed in safety. Skeletons were found of an adult, several youngsters, and some hatchlings in a fossilized nest. The remains of several other dinosaur nests, complete with eggs, lay nearby.

Nesting dinosaurs

The nests were made of heaped-up mounds of mud which had become solid rock. Each nest measured about 10 feet across and five feet high. The nests were about 23 feet apart, leaving just enough room for a mother duckbilled dinosaur to lie beside her eggs. An animal of that size would have been too heavy to sit on her eggs, but she probably kept close guard.

The eggs were laid in a hollow in the middle of the nest mound. In the fossilized nests found, the eggs were arranged in circles,

▲ **Duckbill** dinosaurs probably came back to the same nest site year after year.

▲ **Battling** boneheaded dinosaurs take part in head-butting fights to win mates.

Living in a herd would have been an advantage for dinosaurs, as it is for many animals today, such as zebras. Together, the dinosaurs were safer from predators and they could warn one another of approaching predators or other dangers. At the start of the breeding season, however, rival males would have taken part in fierce battles to decide on the leadership of the herd.

layer on layer. The mother probably covered each layer with earth or sand as she went along and covered the whole nest with earth when she had finished laying eggs. The earth would have keep the eggs warm while they incubated, and well hidden from predators.

By the time the baby dinosaurs struggled out of their eggs they were about 14 inches long. Their mother probably brought them food until they grew strong enough to go and find their own. Since the duckbilled dinosaurs nested in groups, there would always have been some adults around to guard the young while others were away gathering leaves and other food.

Once the young were large enough, they could move with the heard, safe in the protection of the adult animals.

▶ **The egg** of a duckbill dinosaur was about 7 inches long—roughly three times the size of a chicken's egg. It had a tough waterproof shell to protect the growing baby inside.

What went wrong?

When dinosaurs became extinct at the end of the Cretaceous period, 65 million years ago, so did a number of other groups, such as pterosaurs, marine plesiosaurs, and many tiny forms of sea life (plankton). But not all living things were affected. Fish, crocodiles, turtles, birds, mammals, and most flowering plants managed to survive unchanged.

Because these extinctions happened 65 million years ago, no one knows whether they took place over several hundred thousand years, a few thousand years, or within a century. Some scientists think that dinosaurs, and the other groups that became extinct, were becoming less numerous and varied for several million years before the final extinction. They believe that the climate may have become cooler, perhaps because the seas were draining back from the continents and because the many volcanic eruptions at the time were throwing up great quantities of dust into the atmosphere.

▲ **The huge impact** of a large meteorite would have caused earthquakes and tidal waves as well as dust fallout.

Possible impact site

Yucatán

MEXICO

▶ **The Yucatán** area of Mexico may have been the site of the meteorite impact.

◀ **This meteorite crater** is three quarters of a mile wide. The Cretaceous meteorite could have made a crater 150 times this size.

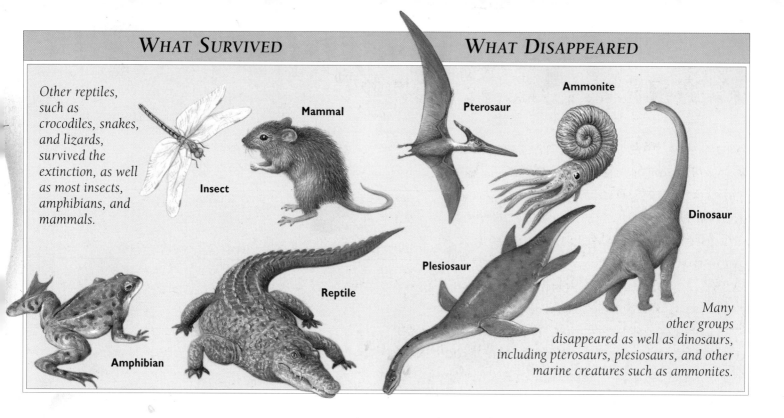

Other reptiles, such as crocodiles, snakes, and lizards, survived the extinction, as well as most insects, amphibians, and mammals.

Insect

Mammal

Pterosaur

Ammonite

Dinosaur

Plesiosaur

Reptile

Amphibian

Many other groups disappeared as well as dinosaurs, including pterosaurs, plesiosaurs, and other marine creatures such as ammonites.

Meteorite impact

But there is also evidence that a great meteorite, measuring some six miles across, struck the Earth at the time of the Cretaceous extinctions. A huge crater that could have been caused by such an impact has been found near the north coast of Mexico. Rocks all over the world laid down at that time contain unusual minerals which could only have come from the material of the meteorite, thrown up into the atmosphere after the enormous impact.

This debris could have darkened the skies for many years, causing a long, cold winter. Many of the plants, both on land and in the sea, would have died from lack of light. Then the plant-eating dinosaurs died in their turn, followed by the carnivorous dinosaurs that ate them.

"Greenhouse effect"

Even after the thicker dust had settled and the long winter ended, the atmosphere would still have contained a lot of finer dust from the rocks thrown up by the force of the impact. These would have caused what scientists call a "greenhouse effect," making the climate much hotter. These two climatic changes would have caused very rapid extinctions, especially of larger animals that needed more food.

It is possible that both groups of scientists are right and the dinosaurs were already becoming less successful before their final end, announced by the fiery glow of a huge meteor streaking across the sky.

▲ **This fossilized shell** belonged to a squidlike creature called an ammonite.

DISCOVERING DINOSAURS

THE LAST DINOSAUR DIED MANY MILLIONS OF YEARS BEFORE IT COULD HAVE been seen and studied by a human being. But modern scientists have at least two ways of finding out about these great animals—first, by comparing them with living animals and, second, by studying their remains.

▼ **Marks where muscles** were attached can be seen on these *Iguanodon* bones.

The evidence

Millions of years ago, dinosaurs had to struggle for survival just like modern animals. They had to find food, defend themselves, and look after their young. Therefore they are likely to have looked and behaved in similar ways to living reptiles and mammals.

The skeleton of a modern animal reveals a great deal about its habits, even without looking at the living creature walking and feeding. A plant eater such as a hippopotamus, for example, has a bulky body, big teeth and heavy jaws for grinding up its food, and short, stocky limbs. When scientists find the bones of a dinosaur with a similar skeleton and teeth, they can feel confident that it, too, had a plant-eating lifestyle. Equally, a dinosaur with pointed teeth, slender limbs, and sharp claws is likely to have been a fast-moving flesh eater that preyed on plant-eating dinosaurs.

▶ **The giant herbivorous dinosaur** known as *Brachiosaurus* had very long front legs and a long neck, giving it a height of more than 42 feet.

Prehistoric giraffe

The structure of the long-necked dinosaur *Brachiosaurus* was similar to that of a modern giraffe. It is therefore likely that *Brachiosaurus* fed in much the same way as today's giraffe, stretching its head up to reach fresh green leaves at the tops of the highest trees.

If you look at the skeleton of a present-day animal, you can see roughened areas on the bones where the muscles were attached. The fossil bones of dinosaurs show similar marks, and these can be compared with the bones of related living animals to help scientists reconstruct the shape of a dinosaur's body and clothe it with flesh.

Dinosaur skin

The really difficult task for scientists reconstructing the appearance of an extinct animal is to figure out what its body covering was like and what color it was. The skin of dinosaurs is believed to have been like that of a crocodile today. It probably had a leathery surface and often contained protective bony lumps.

The colors and patterns of living animals are there to make them invisible to their enemies or their prey, or to allow them to recognize members of their own kind for breeding. Dinosaurs that had similar lifestyles to animals living today may also have had much the same colors and patterns. Color reconstructions of dinosaurs generally use such comparisons with modern animals.

Bone into stone

Most animals live and die without leaving any permanent evidence of their existence. But, occasionally, conditions are suitable for an animal to become fossilized. Imagine that millions of years ago, a duckbilled dinosaur came down to the bank of a lake to drink, but was killed there by a predator. After the carnivore had eaten its fill, most of the flesh and soft tissues were eaten by other scavengers and by insects and the rest slowly rotted away. The skeleton collapsed into a mass of bones that sank into the mud of the river bank. The fossilization process then began.

▲ **The scales that covered the body** of this fossil fish are clearly visible, even though it is more than 35 million years old.

How a fossil forms

As the years went by, each time the river flooded it laid more and more mud above the skeleton until it was deeply buried. The water continued to filter down through the hardening ground, carrying minerals that cemented together the particles of mud and turned it into hard rock. But these minerals also slowly replaced the minerals of the bones of the skeleton and filled up any spaces where the brain cavities and spinal cord had been. Even though the skeleton kept its original shape, it changed into stone.

Over millions of years after the death of the dinosaur, the rocks in which it lay came to lie even deeper in the earth as more mud and sand became deposited on top. But later, the land rose higher. The rocks were then worn away by rain and wind until the skeleton once again lay near to the surface.

Land over much of the world is covered by soil and dense plants. But in deserts, or where a great flood strips away the soil, ancient bones may be seen once more. Even then, only a part of a skeleton may be visible in a cliff face or area of excavation and the rest still lies hidden. Unless someone passes by and recognizes the bones, the fossil may remain undiscovered forever.

Skeletons often become scattered before they are fossilized. Then all that remains are isolated bones, not a complete skeleton. Because the skull is bigger than any of the individual bones, it is often found separately from the rest of the skeleton.

▼ **Stage 1** Just after its death, the dinosaur's bones are still covered by its muscles. Most of its flesh is eaten by carnivores or by other scavenging reptiles, and the rest soon decays.

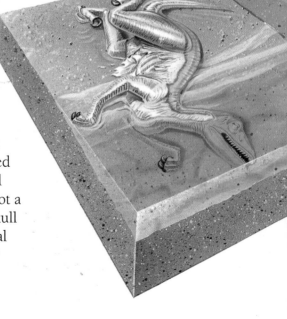

FOSSILIZED TEETH

Fully grown tooth of a flesh-eating dinosaur

Teeth are covered by a layer of hard enamel. They survive well as fossils and can reveal much about the habits of their owner. Long, pointed teeth are found in flesh-eating dinosaurs. Plant eaters, on the other hand, have many smaller teeth for grinding down their food. They grow new teeth to replace old ones as they wear away.

Teeth of a plant-eating dinosaur

Partly grown tooth of a flesh-eating dinosaur

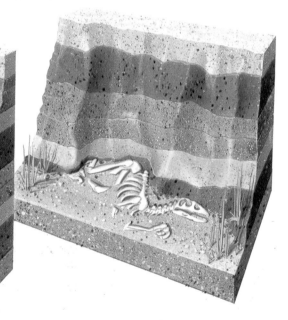

▲ **Stage 2** The dinosaur's skeleton lies on the bed of the lake and sinks into the mud.

▲ **Stage 3** Over millions of years, more layers of lake sediments are deposited above the dinosaur skeleton.

▲ **Stage 4** The land has risen and erosion has started to remove some of the rock above the skeleton.

▲ **Stage 5** Finally, the last layers of rock erode away to reveal the fossil bones.

Digging for dinosaurs

Fossils of dinosaurs and other prehistoric animals are sometimes found by accident. More often they are discovered by paleontologists—scientists who study the life of the past—on special fossil-hunting expeditions. To find remains of Jurassic dinosaurs, for example, paleontologists travel to a part of the world where rocks deposited during the Jurassic period lie on the surface of the Earth. As these rocks are eroded, they may reveal fossil bones that have lain there for millions of years.

Fossil hunting is easiest in desert areas, where plants do not cover the eroding rocks. Even so, paleontologists must spend long days searching for tell-tale glimpses of bone.

▲ **Rock overlying** any part of the fossil skeleton is painstakingly chipped away before a protective coating of plaster of Paris can be applied.

▶ **Freeing a large skeleton** from its rocky home may take a team of people. Tools used range from soft brushes to pickaxes and pneumatic drills.

▲ **Each bone** must be numbered. A plan of the site is made, showing where all the bones lay when found.

Protecting a find

Once a skeleton is found, any rock that lies above it must be carefully removed. The bones cannot simply be lifted from the ground—after millions of years they will be badly cracked and broken. The bones are covered with wet tissue paper, and a layer of sacking, soaked in plaster of Paris, is laid over them. The tissue makes a protective layer between the bones and the sacking so that the sacking does not stick to the bones when it is removed. Once the plaster has hardened, the rock beneath the bones is cut away. The whole section is turned upside down and more plaster is applied to make a jacket around the bones.

Rebuilding a dinosaur

Once safely encased, the fossil bones can be loaded onto a truck or plane for the journey to the museum laboratory. There, scientists strip off the plaster jacket and remove the fossil bones from the rock, using

▲ **A museum worker** models missing pieces of a skeleton using bones from similar skeletons as examples.

Key

Fossil bones

Reconstructed bones

◄ **Only about 60 percent** of the bones of *Baryonyx*, a dinosaur discovered in 1983 in Britain, were ever found. The rest had to be reconstructed.

acids or tiny chisels—a process that can take weeks, or even months. Only then can the rebuilding of the once-living dinosaur begin. It is rare to find all the bones of a skeleton. Usually paleontologists have to restore missing parts, using what they know of similar creatures. The shapes and sizes of the bones can reveal something about the animal's life. Long, slim leg bones,

for example, suggest that an animal was a fast runner.

Finally, the skeleton is mounted and put on display. But fossil bones are delicate and it is often easier to make casts of the original bones from a plastic material. These casts are painted to look like bone and mounted in a lifelike pose. A dinosaur, dead for millions of years, is there for all to see.

Following footprints

Fossilized bones reveal most about the lives of dinosaurs, but information can also be gained from other types of fossils such as footprints, eggs, skin, and even dung.

When dinosaurs came to rivers and lakes to drink, they walked across mud flats, leaving footprints in the mud. Sometimes this would have happened at the beginning of a long spell of dry weather, which baked the surface layer of mud and the footprints. Even if other layers of mud were later laid down on top of it, that layer still remained harder than the rest. Millions of years later, after erosion strips away the softer rocks, this ancient surface with its fossil footprints is once more revealed.

Clues to the past

No one can ever be sure exactly which kind of dinosaur made which fossilized tracks. Guesses can be made by comparing the shape and size of the footprints with the feet of dinosaurs known to have lived in the area when the rocks were deposited. Some tracks give useful clues to the lifestyles of dinosaurs, showing, for example, that they traveled in herds. Smaller footprints in the center of the herd may have belonged to young dinosaurs, protected by the larger and more experienced adults. Other tracks are thought to show the footprints of predatory dinosaurs following herds of larger animals.

Like living reptiles, dinosaurs laid eggs, and fossilized eggs have been found in the same rocks as dinosaur

▲ **The massive footprints** of a dinosaur preserved forever in rock.

bones. For example, nests of the little dinosaur *Protoceratops* have been found in the Gobi Desert. Some of these nests contained more than 30 eggs, each 4 inches long.

An unusual fossil of a duckbilled dinosaur, found in Kansas in the United States, included an imprint of its skin. The dinosaur's body must have dried out after its death in a sandstorm and left its imprint in the sand. Some areas of the skin contain small rounded scales of bone, lying side by side rather than overlapping like the scales of a snake. These scales were bigger on the animal's back and smaller elsewhere.

Other finds include fossilized droppings, known as coprolites. But, as with the footprints, there is no way of knowing exactly what kind of dinosaur such dung came from.

◄ **Like many plant-eating animals** today, such as buffalo, dinosaurs often moved in herds for protection against predators.

▼ **Studying fossilized droppings** gives scientists some information about the diet of dinosaurs.

Dinosaur hunters

▲ A *Diplodocus* skeleton is mounted for exhibition in London in 1905.

It was the great French scientist Georges Cuvier who first realized, 200 years ago, that some fossil remains were so unusual they must belong to creatures no longer living on the Earth. Before then, many people had believed that fossils were the remains of animals still present on Earth, but not yet discovered.

In 1822, a British country doctor named Gideon Mantell described some big teeth that his wife had found in a country lane while he was visiting patients. He thought that they belonged to an extinct relative of the iguana lizard and called the fossil animal *Iguanodon*. Twenty years later, the British paleontologist Richard Owen realized that *Iguanodon* and other huge fossil reptiles belonged to a quite separate group, which he named the dinosaurs.

DINOSAUR RUSH

Intense rivalry to find new types of dinosaurs developed between two collectors—the wealthy Edward Drinker Cope and Professor Othniel Charles Marsh of Yale University (center of back row), who was financed by a rich uncle. Between 1877 and the end of the century, these two scientists described 130 species.

Edward Drinker Cope ▶

New finds

People all over the world became fascinated by these extinct animals and tried to discover more of them.

By the 1850s, dinosaurs such as the duckbilled dinosaur *Hadrosaurus* were being discovered in the United States. As the western parts of the United States were being explored and settled, the eroding rocks of Wyoming, Colorado, and New

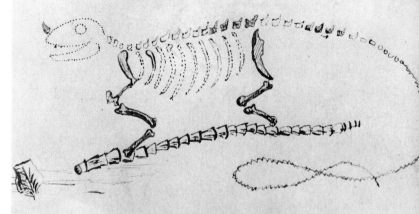

◀ **Dinosaur hunters** on an expedition to the Gobi Desert in the early 1920s.

▲ **Gideon Mantell's sketch** of *Iguanodon*, the dinosaur that he discovered.

Mexico were found to contain the remains of a huge variety of dinosaurs. In one place, the fossil bones were so common that a sheep herder built himself a cabin from the biggest pieces of bone!

Many dinosaurs that had lived near the end of the Cretaceous period were found in Red Deer River Valley in Canada, and were collected by Barnum Brown of the American Museum of Natural History in New York in 1910. Using a specially made barge as a base, he found the remains of many duckbilled and horned dinosaurs. His success encouraged paleontologists from the museum to send expeditions to the Gobi Desert in central Asia between 1922 and 1925. They had hoped to find the remains of early humans, but found instead more remains of Cretaceous dinosaurs.

Now dinosaurs have been found in every continent except Antarctica, where the rocks are mainly covered by snow and ice.

▶ **Barnum Brown**, an American fossil hunter in the early 20th century.

Dinosaur mysteries

Although dinosaurs have been studied for more than 170 years, new species are still being discovered—and we still do not understand everything about the ones that have already been found. Many of the new discoveries are being made in the southern hemisphere in South America, Africa, and Australia, where the rocks are as yet much less explored than in North America and Europe. But sometimes new species are found almost on the doorstep of scientists in the north.

Fish-eating dinosaur

A very unusual dinosaur, named *Baryonyx*, was discovered in Sussex, England by an amateur paleontologist in 1983. The dinosaur is about 28 feet long and has a very strange skull. In most dinosaurs, the skull steadily increases in height from the tip of the snout to the back of the head. But in *Baryonyx* the skull only becomes deep from the level of the eyes backward. The snout is long and low and at the front is a group of large, outwardly pointing large teeth. This type of arrangement of the teeth is not known in any other dinosaur,

▼ The curved claw of *Baryonyx* was nearly 12 inches long. This Early Cretaceous dinosaur may have used its large claws to help it catch fish.

▲ Known only from its 8-foot-long front limbs, *Deinocheirus* was a meat-eating dinosaur of the Late Cretaceous.

but is found in some fish-eating crocodiles and fossil amphibians. These creatures used their teeth to impale fish. A big curved claw was also found with the skeleton of *Baryonyx*. The dinosaur may have used this claw to pierce fish and hold them down while it ate.

An even more remarkable dinosaur lived in Mongolia toward the end of the Cretaceous period. Paleontologists would love to know more about it, but all that has been found so far are its enormous arms which are nearly 8 feet long. These arms give the dinosaur its name, *Deinocheirus*, which means "terrible hand." The arms are slender, similar to those of ornithomimids (*see pages 42–43*), but are much longer and end in three fingers that bear huge, 12-inch claws. Unlike ornithomimids, *Deinocheirus* could not have folded its fingers back to grasp its food. The way of life of this strange dinosaur will remain mysterious until a more complete skeleton is found.

In addition to completely new, or incompletely known, dinosaurs, more is still being discovered about some of the dinosaurs that were found long ago. Part of the fascination of dinosaurs is the unimaginably great size of some of them, and no one knows just how big the largest of them were. Until recently, the biggest of the great plant-eating dinosaurs called sauropods were thought to have been creatures such as *Camarasaurus* and *Brachiosaurus* (*see pages 40–41*). But over the past 20 years, the remains of larger and larger sauropods have been found that may have been more than 100 feet long. They have been given names such as *Supersaurus*, *Ultrasaurus*, and *Seismosaurus*.

▶ **This model** shows how *Baryonyx* may have looked at just before it died.

◀ **Some paleontologists believe** that *Baryonyx* was a scavenger which followed carnivorous dinosaurs and ate what was left from their kills.

THE RULING REPTILES

THE JURASSIC AND CRETACEOUS PERIODS WERE THE AGE OF THE RULING reptiles, when the dinosaurs were most diverse and numerous and they dominated the land. Mammals had evolved by this time, but were mostly small creatures the size of field mice or chipmunks.

Dinosaur family tree

There were probably about 400 different types of dinosaurs, ranging from the gigantic plant-eating sauropods to fast-running predators. The diagram here shows the two major groups of dinosaurs—the ornithischians and the saurischians (*see pages 12–13*)—and the main families in each of the groups. Each family contained many species. For example, the hadrosaur family included the dinosaur *Lambeosaurus* (*see pages 48–49*) and about 10 other known genera, or types.

Carnosaurs

Ornithomimids

Dromaeosaurs

Birds

Ornitholestes

Gallimimus

Dromaeosaurus

Archeopteryx

Tyrannosaurus

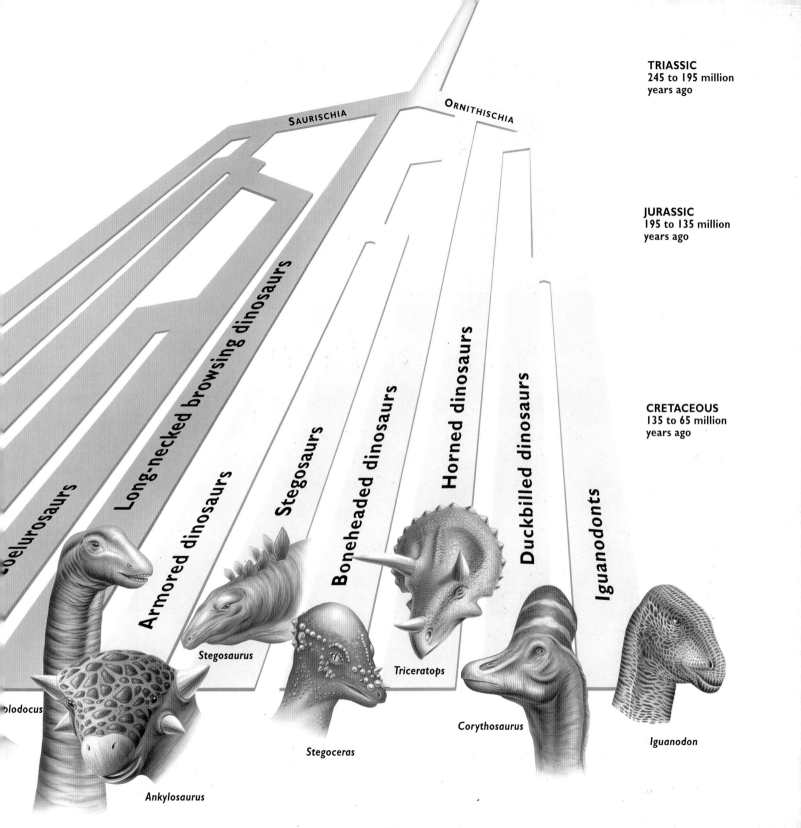

SAURISCHIA

ORNITHISCHIA

TRIASSIC
245 to 195 million
years ago

JURASSIC
195 to 135 million
years ago

CRETACEOUS
135 to 65 million
years ago

Coelurosaurs

Long-necked browsing dinosaurs

Armored dinosaurs

Stegosaurs

Boneheaded dinosaurs

Horned dinosaurs

Duckbilled dinosaurs

Iguanodonts

Diplodocus

Ankylosaurus

Stegosaurus

Stegoceras

Triceratops

Corythosaurus

Iguanodon

Long-necked browsing dinosaurs

Between 65 and 200 million years ago, the largest herbivores were the giant, long-necked browsing dinosaurs called sauropods. In fact, these were the largest land animals ever to have lived. Even in the early stages of their evolution, most sauropods were well over 50 feet long. All had a small head on top of an extra-long neck, a deep body to hold the enormous stomach, thick, pillarlike legs, and a long tail which tapered to a whiplash.

▲ *Camarasaurus* had chisel-shaped teeth, which it used to strip leaves from trees.

▲ **The neck of *Diplodocus*** was at least 23 feet long, but its head was tiny for such a large animal. At less than 2 feet long, it was not much bigger than a horse's head.

Brachiosaurs

The monsters of this giant group were the brachiosaurs. They lived in North America, Europe, and Africa during Mid-Jurassic to Early Cretaceous times. All had the typical sauropod body structure, but they differed in having front legs that were longer than their back legs, so that the body sloped down from the shoulders, like that of a modern giraffe (see pages 24–25).

Brachiosaurus was long thought to have been the most massive dinosaur ever to have lived, but finds in North America have shown that there were even larger sauropods. In 1986, for example, huge dinosaur bones were unearthed in New Mexico. This sauropod has been named *Seismosaurus* and may have been as much as 120 feet long.

Diplodocids were as long or longer than brachiosaurs, but much lighter. The special structure of their vertebrae (the bones that make up the backbone) made them light for their size. These bones were partly hollow, so they weighed less than if they were made of solid bone but were still just as strong. *Diplodocus*, for example, weighed only about 11 tons, far less than *Brachiosaurus*,

SAUROPODS

Order: **Saurischia**

Families: **Cetiosauridae, Brachiosauridae, Camarasauridae, Diplodocidae, Titanosauridae**

Time: **Jurassic and Cretaceous**
Size: **21–120 feet long**

Fossils found in: **Worldwide except Antarctica**

Brachiosaurus

Camarasaurus

which probably weighed in at an amazing 80 tons, as much as 12 African elephants today.

Diplodocids may have been able to rear up on their hind legs, using the long tail to help support the body. This would have helped them to reach up to the highest leaves. Diplodocids may also have been able to rear up to defend themselves against enemies. Only the biggest hunters, such as *Allosaurus*, the largest meat eater of the time, would have dared attack such giants.

Camarasaurs were smaller than brachiosaurs and diplodocids, and had shorter necks and tails. The two other sauropod families, cetiosaurs and titanosaurs, are less well known than the others. Small for sauropods, the biggest titanosaurs were only 50 feet long.

▶ **Camarasaurs** and brachiosaurs were both common in the Late Jurassic period. *Camarasaurus* was 59 feet long and weighed 20 tons. These creatures moved in herds across the tropical plains of western North America, searching for plants to eat. *Brachiosaurus* lived in North America and Africa.

39

Small carnivorous dinosaurs

Ceratosaurs, coelurosaurs, and oviraptors were the smallest of the flesh-eating dinosaurs.

The most primitive of these were the ceratosaurs, a group which includes many dinosaurs from the Late Triassic and Early Jurassic periods. Most were very active predators, with powerful arms and strongly clawed hands and feet. *Saltopus*, one of the smallest dinosaurs so far discovered, was a ceratosaur. It was smaller than a domestic cat and probably weighed only a couple of pounds. Like most of this group, its lightness was due to the fact that many of its bones were thin-walled and hollow.

▶ **The coelurosaur** *Ornitholestes* caught prey such as lizards and frogs in its sharp-clawed hands.

Built for speed
A much larger ceratosaur was *Coelophysis*, which may have been up to 10 feet long. Despite its size, its hollow bones meant that it probably only weighed 50 pounds. This early dinosaur must have been a ferocious hunter and was built for speed.

The long narrow jaws were equipped with many sharp teeth, each with a cutting, serrated edge. There were four fingers on each hand, though only three were strong enough to grasp prey. A number of fossil skeletons of *Coelophysis* were found in New Mexico in 1947. These included very young individuals as well as adults. Finding all these animals in one place suggests that they lived as a group and all died together.

Coelurosaurs were also fast-moving, lightly built hunters, with hollow bones. Best known is *Coelurus*, a predator which lived in the forests and swamps of North America. It had a small head, slender limbs, and hands with three sharp-clawed fingers for grasping prey.

The oviraptors lived in eastern Asia during the Late Cretaceous

Oviraptor

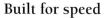

Saltopus

◀ **Small carnivores,** such as *Saltopus* and *Oviraptor*, all walked upright on their hind legs, leaving their hands free for grasping prey.

▶ Packs of *Coelophysis* may have roamed forests, hunting for prey such as the small, shrewlike mammals that evolved at the end of the Triassic.

SMALL CARNIVOROUS DINOSAURS

Order: **Saurischia**

Families: **Ceratosauria, Coelurosauria, Oviraptosauria**

Time: **Triassic, Jurassic, and Cretaceous**

Size: **2–20 feet long**

Fossils found in: **Worldwide except Antarctica**

period. They had short heads with toothless jaws and a heavy beak. The name of these dinosaurs means "egg-thief" because the first *Oviraptor* fossil was discovered with a clutch of eggs. At first it was thought that these eggs had been laid by the horned dinosaur *Protoceratops* (*see pages 18–19*) and that *Oviraptor* had died while raiding the nest. In fact, it has now been discovered that the eggs belonged to *Oviraptor*.

◀ Coelurus preyed on lizards, flying reptiles, and other small animals.

41

Dromaeosaurs and Ornithomimids

Intelligent and fast moving, dromaeosaurs and ornithomimids were highly successful hunters in Late Cretaceous times. Dromaeosaurs had the light, speedy body of a coelurosaur (*see pages 40–41*), but with a more formidable head and jaws. They probably hunted in packs. With their long narrow beaks, ornithomimids looked very like today's flightless birds, such as ostriches. Like ostriches, these long-legged dinosaurs traveled in groups, searching for food.

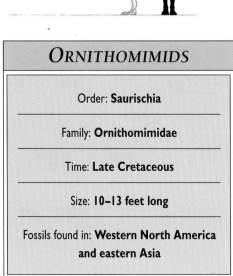

Gallimimus

Struthiomimus

Ornithomim…

ORNITHOMIMIDS
Order: **Saurischia**
Family: **Ornithomimidae**
Time: **Late Cretaceous**
Size: **10–13 feet long**
Fossils found in: **Western North America and eastern Asia**

▲ **Ornithomimids** did not have big claws or strong teeth to protect themselves from attackers, but few other dinosaurs could catch them when they ran at full speed.

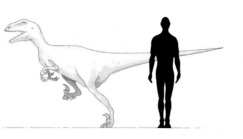

◀ **The sharp, sickle claw** on each foot of a dromaeosaur was about 5 inches long.

DROMAEOSAURS

Order: **Saurischia**

Family: **Dromaeosauridae**

Time: **Mid to Late Cretaceous**

Size: **6–13 feet long**

Fossils found in: **Western Europe and eastern Asia**

Adaptable hunters

Ornithomimids had large eyes and big brains, which would have helped make them efficient hunters. Like ostriches today, they probably had a varied diet, including fruit and berries, as well as insects and other small animals. They may also have dug into the ground to find and eat eggs buried by other dinosaurs, pecking through the shells with their hard beaks.

Ornithomimus was typical of the ornithomimids, with its small head, beaklike jaws, and no teeth. It could probably run at up to 40 miles an hour, holding the long tail straight out behind its body to help to balance the head and neck. The clawed hands were held ready to grasp any food that came its way.

Dromaeosaurs had a lethal weapon in the form of a large, sickle-shaped claw on the second toe of each foot. This could have been used like a dagger to slash through the victim's flesh as the dromaeosaur stood on one leg and kicked with its free foot. When a dromaeosaur ran, the sickle claws on its toes were held clear of the ground. Each hand was equipped with three long fingers, tipped with strong claws for seizing hold of prey.

Perhaps the best known dromaeosaur is *Deinonychus,* which was about 10 feet long and stood about 6 feet tall. Working in packs, these dinosaurs could attack prey much bigger than themselves. A group of *Deinonychus* could have overcome a large plant-eating dinosaur, some leaping on its back and holding on with their clawed hands, while others surrounded it, slashing its thick hide with the claws on their feet.

▶ *Deinonychus* **had** a large head and powerful jaws. Its teeth curved backward and had jagged edges for cutting into the thick skin of prey.

Carnosaurs

The biggest carnivorous dinosaurs, known as carnosaurs, were heavily built creatures, with big heads and jaws lined with daggerlike teeth. The arms and two-clawed hands of a typical carnosaur were surprisingly small for the huge body. Some experts think that the animal may have used its arms to lift itself up off the ground after sleeping or feeding. Most carnosaurs had a short powerful neck. This was important not only for supporting the head, but also for wrenching the head from side to side to tear chunks of flesh away from victims.

CARNOSAURS
Order: **Saurischia**
Families: **Allosauridae, Tyrannosauridae, Spinosauridae**
Time: **Early Jurassic to Late Cretaceous**
Size: **Up to 50 feet long and 20 feet tall**
Fossils found: **Worldwide except Antarctica and Australia**

▼ A mighty predator, the carnosaur *Allosaurus* stood up to 15 feet tall and must have weighed between 1 and 2 tons.

▶ Yangchuanosaurus was a typical carnosaur with a powerful head and body and huge, pillarlike back legs.

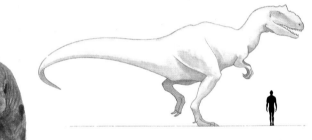

Hunters or scavengers?
Allosaurs were the largest carnosaurs during the Late Jurassic. *Allosaurus*, for example, was up to 39 feet long. Some paleontologists think that this dinosaur would have been too heavy and clumsy to chase prey, and may have fed on carrion, the remains of dead animals, instead. Others think that it might have been able to move quite fast for short distances and could have hunted in packs to bring down the giant plant eaters of the day, such as *Apatosaurus* and *Diplodocus*. *Apatosaurus* bones bearing the marks of teeth similar to

those of *Allosaurus* have been found in western North America.

Spinosaurs and tyrannosaurs lived during the Cretaceous. The largest of these carnosaurs was the mighty *Tyrannosaurus*, which stood up to 20 feet tall and weighed about 8 tons—more than an African elephant today. Like all carnosaurs, it ran on its two back legs, holding the long tail straight out behind it to balance the weight of the head and front of the body.

It has been suggested that *Tyrannosaurus*, like *Allosaurus*, may have been a scavenger and not a fierce hunter at all. However, many experts believe that the structure of its head and teeth suggest that it was an active predator. *Tyrannosaurus* probably fed mostly on duckbilled dinosaurs (*see pages 48–49*) which browsed in the forests of North America. These animals lived in herds and were always on the watch for danger, sprinting away when alarmed. *Tyrannosaurus* may have hidden among trees and waited for victims to come near. It could then leap out and seize its prey in its strong jaws.

But *Tyrannosaurus* may not have been the biggest predatory dinosaur. In 1995 the skull of a meat eater was found in North Africa. This dinosaur, named *Carcharodontosaurus*, may have been even larger and heavier than *Tyrannosaurus*.

▲ *Tyrannosaurus* probably ambushed prey, charging toward its victim with its huge jaws open and ready to bite.

Iguanodonts

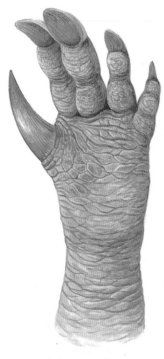

▲ Iguanodon may have used its thumb spike to defend itself against attackers.

Large, plant-eating dinosaurs, iguanodonts evolved in the Jurassic period and spread throughout the world. Their remains have even been found within what is now the Arctic Circle—the area would have been ice-free at that time. Iguanodonts were bulky, big-boned animals, with sturdy legs and hooflike nails on their feet. Probably fairly slow-moving, they would have spent most of their time on all-fours browsing on low-growing plants. They could also rear up on to their hind legs to reach leaves higher in the trees.

▲ Ouranosaurus lived in the Sahara area of North Africa.

◀ Muttaburrasaurus is one of the few dinosaurs so far found in Australia.

"Iguana tooth"

Iguanodonts are named after the most famous member of the family, *Iguanodon,* which was the second dinosaur to be discovered (*see pages 32–33*). Part of a leg bone was found in England in 1809, and more bones and some teeth in 1822. Gideon Mantell, a fossil hunter and one of the discoverers of these remains, realized that the teeth belonged to a reptile and looked something like those of modern iguana lizards. He named the animal *Iguanodon,* which means "iguana tooth." The term "dinosaur" had not been invented.

Iguanodon stood about 16 feet tall and probably weighed about 5 tons. It had a long head ending in a powerful, toothless beak used for chopping off mouthfuls of leaves. Farther back in the jaws were strong teeth for chewing tough plants.

The legs were long and pillarlike, each with three stout toes tipped with heavy, hooflike nails. Each short arm had a five-fingered hand, which could be spread wide and used for walking when the animal was on all-fours. Instead of a thumb, *Iguanodon* had a sharp thumb spike that stuck out sideways from the hand. In the first reconstructions of this dinosaur, the spike was placed on its nose, like

▲ At 30 feet long, *Iguanodon* was the largest of its family.

◄ *Iguanodon* could move on all fours and rear up on its hind legs.

a horn. Three of the other fingers had hooflike nails. The fifth finger could be bent across the palm and used to grasp food.

Iguanodon has left its footprints in the rocks of southern England. These great tracks suggest that the animals traveled in herds. Similar footprints have been found in South America and in the Arctic Circle.

Other members of the family lived in a similar way. One unusual iguanodont was *Ouranosaurus*. It had a row of spines running down the center of its back, from its shoulders to halfway along the tail. These were covered with skin to form a finlike structure. *Ouranosaurus* also had a wide flat snout and two bony bumps on its skull. These were similar to the low crests of hadrosaurs (*see pages 48–49*). Another iguanodont, *Muttaburrasaurus* had similar bumps on its head.

47

Duckbilled dinosaurs

The duckbilled dinosaurs, or hadrosaurs, were among the most common and varied of all groups of dinosaurs. They probably evolved in central Asia, and by the Late Cretaceous had spread all over the northern hemisphere. Many of these plant-eating dinosaurs had strangely shaped crests or bumps on their heads. But their most characteristic feature was the way that the front of the face formed a long, flattened beak. This was similar to the beak of a duck and has given the group its common name.

▲ **Lambeosaurus** had a bony spike behind its tall head crest.

Successful dinosaurs

A hadrosaur's beak was toothless, but there were large teeth farther back in the jaws for chewing a wide variety of plants, including tough pine needles, magnolia leaves, seeds, and fruits of all kinds. New teeth grew continually to replace old worn ones.

All hadrosaurs had long back legs and shorter front legs. They probably spent most of their time feeding on all fours, but when they had to run quickly to escape from predators, they probably reared up on their back legs and sprinted away. Most had a flexible neck, allowing them to reach around the body and gather plenty of low-growing plants from a wide area without having to move too much.

▲ **Parasaurolophus** had a backward-pointing, hornlike crest on its head that measured up to 6 feet long. The crest may have fitted into a notch in the dinosaur's backbone when the head was held up.

Some hadrosaurs had flat heads, while others had crests on the top of their heads. Different species had crests of different shapes, and it is possible that the crests of males and females of the same species varied in shape and size. Hollow passages inside the crest may have acted like echo chambers to make the hadrosaurs' booming calls even louder. The shape of the crest altered the sound made, so each kind of hadrosaur may have had its own call.

Hadrosaurs lived in herds, and the crests and calls could have helped them to recognize and keep in touch with others of their kind, as well as find mates. Remains of hadrosaur eggs show that these dinosaurs also nested in groups and may have shared the care of their young (*see pages 20–21*).

HADROSAURS
Order: **Ornithischia**
Family: **Hadrosauridae**
Time: **Late Cretaceous**
Size: **12–43 feet long**
Fossils found: **North and South America, Europe, and Asia**

Corythosaurus

Edmontosaurus

Shantungosaurus

▲ **Among the largest** of the hadrosaurs was *Shantungosaurus* at about 43 feet long.

▲ **The long, deep tails** of hadrosaurs helped balance the weight of the front of the body when the animals ran upright on two legs.

Horned dinosaurs

The most abundant plant-eating dinosaurs in western North America during the Late Cretaceous were the ceratopians, or horned dinosaurs.

These creatures were extremely well armored. Typically a horned dinosaur had a massive head armed with a sharp, parrrotlike beak at the front; long, pointed horns on the brow or snout, or sometimes both; and a great sheet of bone, called a frill, which grew out from the back of the skull and curved upward. This protected the dinosaur's neck and shoulders.

▲ **Centrosaurus** had a strong neck and shoulders to help support the weight of its massive head.

▼ **If threatened,** adult *Triceratops* dinosaurs would form a ring around the young in the herd and shake their great heads at the enemy.

Short frills and long frills

The success of the horned dinosaurs was largely due to their powerful beaklike jaws and chopping teeth. They could have eaten the toughest of plant foods, including the flowering plants that had only begun to thrive during the Late Cretaceous. The dinosaurs probably moved in great herds through the forests, chopping mouthfuls of plants with their sharp, toothless beaks.

There were two groups of horned dinosaurs, one with short neck frills and the other with long neck frills. Typical of the short-frilled group was *Centrosaurus*. Its neck frill was fringed with spines, and it had one long horn on its snout and two short horns on its brow. Like all horned dinosaurs, it had pillarlike legs supporting a heavy body covered in thick hide.

Chasmosaurus was a typical long-frilled horned dinosaur. It had a long, narrow skull, with a pair of curving horns on the brow and single shorter horn on the snout. The bony frill was enormous, stretching from the back of the skull to cover the neck and upper shoulders.

Such spectacular frills must have acted as a warning to enemies, either predators or rival males. Few animals would risk attacking such an impressive opponent. If necessary, ceratopians could use their sharp horns to defend themselves against enemies.

▼ **The mighty neck frill** of *Chasmosaurus* was studded with bony spikes and knobs, making the animal look even more threatening.

◄ **In addition to three horns,** *Pentaceratops* had bony growths projecting from its cheek bones.

CERATOPIANS

Order: **Ornithischia**

Family: **Ceratopidae**

Time: **Late Cretaceous**

Size: **6–30 feet long**

Fossils found in: **Western North America**

▼ *Triceratops* was abut 30 feet long and the largest horned dinosaur.

Boneheaded dinosaurs

The most unusual features of the so-called boneheaded dinosaurs were their dome-shaped skulls. The skull was protected by a thickened dome of bone, which acted as a built-in crash helmet. Some species also had bony frills, knobs, and spikes on the back and sides of the head, and sometimes on the snout. Female boneheads had smaller, thinner skulls than males.

These dinosaurs may have had a lifestyle like that of modern mountain goats. Like the goats, these dinosaurs lived together in herds. Males probably took part in fierce battles during the mating season.

▲ The jaws
of *Stegoceras* contained slightly curved, jagged-edged teeth, ideally shaped for tearing up plant food.

▲The bony dome
on top of the head of *Stegoceras* may have been boldly colored, as shown here.

Head-butting fighters

Boneheaded dinosaurs were plant eaters. They walked on two legs and had five-fingered hands, three-toed feet, and a long heavy tail. Most of those so far discovered lived during the Late Cretaceous period in North America and Asia, but one bonehead has been found in Early Cretaceous rocks in southern England.

The two families of boneheaded dinosaurs were the homalocephalids and the pachycephalosaurs. The homocephalids did not have such highly domed heads as the pachycephalosaurs, although the bones of the skull were greatly thickened and their heads were covered with many bony knobs.

Rival males may have fought ritual, head-butting battles similar to those of the marine iguanas on the Galápagos Islands today. The homalocephalids also had unusually broad hips, leading some paleontologists to believe that these dinosaurs gave birth to live young, instead of laying eggs. Others think that the broad hips took some of the impact when the dinosaurs fought.

Pachycephalosaurs had much more highly domed skulls, and on some species the dome was ringed with spikes. The domes of males grew larger with age.

Although they were peaceful creatures for most of the time, rival male pachycephalosaurs, such as *Stegoceras*, fought to win females during the mating season. They charged toward one another with head lowered and neck, body, and tail held straight out. The tail would have helped to balance the weight of the head. The domed area of the skull would have taken most of the impact as the animals crashed head-on into each other.

Boneheaded dinosaurs probably had large eyes and a keen sense of smell. They fed on leaves and fruits.

▼ **The skull of** *Pachycephalosaurus* was about 2 feet long. The enormous dome on the top was made of solid bone, up to 10 inches thick.

BONEHEADED DINOSAURS

Order: **Ornithischia**

Families: **Pachycepthalosauridae, Homalocephalidae**

Time: **Early to Late Cretaceous**

Size: **6–26 feet long**

Fossils found in: **North America, Madagascar, Europe, and Asia**

▼ ***Homalocephale*** lived in Asia during the Late Cretaceous and was about 10 feet long.

Armored dinosaurs

During the Cretaceous period, heavily armored dinosaurs called ankylosaurs and nodosaurs spread through the northern continents. Typically, the neck, back, sides, and tail of an armored dinosaur were entirely covered with flat plates of bones set into the thick skin. Spikes and knobs also studded the body armor.

The nodosaurs were the earlier and more primitive of the two families. They had narrow skulls, armored backs, and long spikes sticking out of their sides. The ankylosaurs had broad skulls and a heavy "club" of bone at the end of the tail.

▲ Short horns at the back of the skull of *Euoplocephalus* gave the head extra protection.

Defense against danger

The largest of the nodosaurs was *Sauropelta*. About 25 feet long, the body of this massive dinosaur was encased in bony armor, and it probably weighed more than 3 tons. This armor consisted of bands of plates of bone which ran over the body from neck to the end of the long, tapering tail. Any attacker was further discouraged by the row of sharp spikes that stuck out from each

◄ Euoplocephalus lived in North America during the Late Cretaceous. If attacked, this ankylosaur would lash out with its clublike tail.

▼ **If in danger** *Sauropelta* would stay still and rely on its armor for defense.

ARMORED DINOSAURS

Order: **Ornithischia**

Families: **Ankylosauridae, Nodosauridae**

Time: **Mid Jurassic to Late Cretaceous**

Size: **13–20 feet long**

Fossils found in: **North America, Europe, Asia, and Australia**

▲ *Panoplosaurus* may have charged its attackers rather than simply relying on its armor for protection.

side of the body. A slow-moving creature, *Sauropelta* needed its armor to protect itself from attacks by meat-eating dinosaurs.

Another nodosaur, *Panoplosaurus,* even had bony plates on its head and massive spikes guarding its shoulders. This dinosaur may have used its spiked shoulders to defend itself against attackers.

Ankylosaurs were even more heavily armored than nodosaurs. Even their eyelids were protected—pieces of bone came down like shutters over the normal lids to protect their eyes from sharp claws. A predator's only chance was to try to turn the ankylosaur over onto its back. The undersides were less well protected than the rest of the body. Ankylosaurs also had a unique weapon in the form of a bony club at the end of the tail. This could seriously injure even a large predator such as *Tyrannosaurus*. The club was made up of two large balls of bone joined together. The bones of the tail were stiffened and strengthened with thin bony rods to help support the heavy club.

The largest of the ankylosaurs was *Ankylosaurus*, which lived in North America. Built like a tank, it probably weighed at least 4 tons. Like all ankylosaurs, it had a blunt snout and a toothless beak for chopping off mouthfuls of plant food.

Stegosaurs

The double rows of bony plates along the back made these some of the most distinctive of all dinosaurs. Typically, a stegosaur had a small head, huge body, and a heavy tail armed with pairs of long, sharp spikes. Like iguanodonts (*see pages 46–47*) and duckbilled dinosaurs (*see pages 48–49*), stegosaurs were plant eaters and probably lived in herds. But, unlike their more agile relatives, stegosaurs moved on four legs and could not rear up and run fast on two to escape enemies. When attacked, a stegosaur would probably have stood its ground and lashed out with its long, spiked tail.

STEGOSAURS	
Order: **Ornithischia**	
Family: **Stegosauridae**	
Time: **Mid Jurassic to Late Cretaceous**	
Size: **10–30 feet long**	
Fossils found: **North America, Europe, Africa, and Asia**	

Bony body plates

Stegosaurus is the most familiar of the stegosaurs. The broad, bony plates on its back were shaped like huge arrowheads. They ran down each side of the backbone, from just behind the head to halfway along the tail.

No one is sure exactly how the bony plates were arranged on *Stegosaurus*. Although many well-preserved skeletons have been found, none have had the plates still attached to the body. Some paleontologists believe that the plates lay flat on the body and formed protective armor

▶ **The largest** plates on *Stegosaurus* were nearly 2 feet tall.

▲ **Stegosaurus** was as much as 30 feet long and the biggest stegosaur so far discovered.

for the animal. Most, however, now think that the plates stood upright and were arranged in two alternating rows, as shown here. They would have still helped to protect the stegosaur, making it more difficult to attack.

There is also a theory that the plates were a way of controlling body temperature. Blood-rich skin may have covered the plates. When a stegosaur was cold, it could have turned one side toward the sun. The sun's heat could then warm the blood as it passed over the plates on its way around the body. When turned away from the sun and into a breeze, the plates could have given off heat and thus cooled the animal.

Stegosaurus was about 20 feet long. Its massive back legs were more than twice the length of the front legs, which meant that the body sloped forward from the hips. The skull was tiny—only about 16 inches long—and housed a brain the size of a walnut. There was a toothless beak at the front of the jaws and some small weak teeth farther back.

Stegosaurus

▶ **The stegosaur** *Kentrosaurus* lived in Africa. It was about 16 feet long and had narrower bony plates than *Stegosaurus*.

Kentrosaurus

57

Flying reptiles

The first vertebrates (animals with backbones) to take to life in the air were the pterosaurs. These flying reptiles flew on wings made of skin and attached to extra long fingers on each hand. Pterosaurs evolved in the Late Triassic, about 70 million years before the first-known bird, *Archaeopteryx*, appeared. They became extinct at the end of the Cretaceous at the same time as the dinosaurs. In size, pterosaurs ranged from small species about the size of a blackbird to the largest flying creatures ever.

PTEROSAURS
Suborders: **Rhamphorhynchoidea, Pterodactyloidea**
Time: **Late Triassic to Late Cretaceous**
Size: **Wingspan up to 39 feet**
Fossils found: **Worldwide**

▼ **No one knows** how pterosaurs moved on the ground. Some experts think that they crawled along using the claws on their wings as well as their feet.

◀ The earliest known bird, Archaeopteryx lived 150 million years ago and had features of both reptiles and birds. Like reptiles, it had toothed jaws and a long, bony tail. Like birds, it had feathers and wings.

▼ With a wingspan of 45 feet Quetzalcoatlus was the biggest pterodactyl. Ramphorhynchs were smaller with wingspans of up to 4 feet.

▲ A pterodactyl, Pteranodon had a wingspan of up to 23 feet. It proably glided above the ocean on its huge wings, searching for fish to snap up.

Pterodactyls and rhamphorhynchs

There were two kinds of flying reptiles—rhamphorhynchs and pterodactyls. All had wings attached to the enormously elongated fourth finger of each hand. The other three fingers were short and tipped with sharp claws. The wings were also attached to the sides of the pterosaur's body, possibly at about hip level. Scientists believe that pterosaurs did actually flap their wings, rather than just gliding through the air. Recent research shows that the wings may have been strengthened by tough fibers.

Rhamphorhynchs were the earliest and most primitive pterosaurs. They had short legs and a long bony tail which made up about half the animal's length. This tail would have been held straight out during flight and may have helped to balance the front part of the body. Typically, rhamphorhynchs had large heads and jaws filled with sharp teeth.

Pterodactyls developed during the Jurassic. They had the same general structure as the rhamphorhynchs, but the tail was shorter and the neck and skull longer.

Pterosaurs may have fed in a variety of ways. Some of the smaller, fast-flying pterosaurs probably chased prey in mid-air, like today's insect-eating birds. Others, such as *Pterodactylus*, snatched fish from the water in its long, narrow jaws. *Pteranodon* was an unusual pterosaur because it had no teeth. It may have fed by scooping up fish and swallowing them whole.

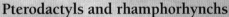

Marine reptiles

During the reign of the dinosaurs on land, some groups of reptiles became adapted to life in the sea. Most successful were the long-necked plesiosaurs and the fishlike ichthyosaurs. These creatures dominated the world's seas for more than 100 million years during the Jurassic and Cretaceous periods.

Plesiosaurs were large creatures, up to 46 feet long, with sturdy bodies, short tails, and long narrow flippers, similar in shape to those of penguins and turtles today. Paleontologists used to think that plesiosaurs made rowing movements with their flippers, but most now believe that they flapped them up and down, enabling them to "fly" through the water.

The plesiosaurs fed on fish and squid. Their long necks meant they could raise their head high above the surface of the sea and search the waves for signs of prey.

▲ *Elasmosaurus* was the longest known plesiosaur at 46 feet. More than half its total length was neck.

▲ **A powerful hunter**
Kronosaurus was the largest known pliosaur. Its flat-topped skull alone measured 9 feet.

Tigers of the sea
Pliosaurs were closely related to the long-necked plesiosaurs. These marine reptiles had shorter necks than plesiosaurs but much larger heads and jaws, equipped with strong teeth. They could catch bigger prey than plesiosaurs and became the tigers of the Jurassic seas, chasing and overpowering large

▲ **At 49 feet long**
Shonisaurus was the longest known ichthyosaur.

▲ **The ichthyosaur**
Ophthalmosaurus chased prey in the water and seized it in its strong jaws.

▼**The paddlelike fins**
of ichthyosaurs were used for steering as they swam.

ICHTHYOSAURS

Order: **Ichthyosauria**

Time: **Early Triassic to Mid Cretaceous**

Size: **Up to 49 feet long**

Fossils found: **Worldwide**

PLESIOSAURS

Superfamily: **Plesiosauroidea**

Time: **Early Jurassic to late Cretaceous**

Size: **Up to 46 feet long**

Fossils found: **Worldwide**

PLIOSAURS

Superfamily: **Pliosauroidea**

Time: **Early Jurassic to Late Cretaceous**

Size: **Up to 42 feet long**

Fossils found: **Worldwide**

sea creatures such as sharks and large squid.

Plesiosaurs spent nearly all their lives at sea, but came to land to lay eggs, just like turtles do today. They dragged themselves up onto a beach and laid their eggs in pits that they made in the sand. When the young hatched, they made their own way down to the sea.

Best adapted of all marine reptiles were the ichthyosaurs. Although they were air-breathing reptiles, they had a streamlined, fishlike body and a tail that provided the main force for swimming, just like the tail of a modern shark or tuna.

Ichthyosaurs lived much like today's dolphins, cruising the seas at high speed and hunting prey such as

fish and squid. They did not come ashore to lay eggs, but gave birth to live young at sea.

Like other marine reptiles, ichthyosaurs had to come to the surface at regular intervals to breathe air. The nostrils were set high up on the skull so that the animal did not have to lift its head far out of the water to take a breath.

Other reptiles

Reptiles first evolved in the Late Carboniferous period about 300 million years ago. Many different groups thrived before the archosaurs, or ruling reptiles, which included the dinosaurs, pterosaurs, and crocodiles, began to dominate. Among the earliest reptiles were the procolophonids which lived until the Late Triassic. *Hypsognathus*, one of the later members of this family, was probably a plant eater. It had a wide, squat body and broad cheek teeth suitable for grinding tough plants. An array of spikes around its head would have helped protect it against predators.

▲ **A long-legged lizard,** *Kuehneosaurus,* could glide from tree to tree on flaps of skin at the sides of its body.

◄ **The rhynchosaur** *Hyperodapedon* lived during the Late Triassic. It chopped mouthfuls of plants with its strong teeth.

▶ **Hypsognathus** lived in North America during the Late Triassic. It was about 13 inches long.

Early turtles

Another group of the earliest reptiles still survives today—the chelonians, which includes turtles and tortoises. They differ from other reptiles in having their bodies, except for the head, tail, and legs, enclosed within a shell. Even the earliest chelonians had a shell; in fact, turtles and tortoises have hardly changed over the last 200 million years. The sea turtle *Archelon*, which lived in the Late Cretaceous seas, had a light shell made up of a framework of bony ribs. This was probably covered by a thick coat of rubbery skin. Its limbs were like huge paddles which it would have used to push itself through the water. Although they lived in the sea and looked like turtles, placodonts, such as *Placochelys*, were a separate group. Bony plates covered the back of *Placochelys*, and it had paddlelike limbs for swimming.

Phytosaurs were the dominant predators in rivers during the Triassic. These heavily armored crocodilelike creatures had long snouts and jaws filled with sharp teeth, ideal for preying on fish.

Lizards and snakes lived alongside the dinosaurs, but survived the mass extinction at the end of the Cretaceous (*see pages 22–23*). Among the earliest known lizards was *Kuehneosaurus*, which could glide through the air on "wings" made of skin at the sides of its body.

Some of the most common reptiles in the Triassic were rhynchosaurs, such as *Hyperodapedon*, which feasted on seed ferns that were plentiful at that time. But these plants died out at the end of that period and were replaced by conifers. The rhynchosaurs then died out, too, and were replaced by the newly evolved, plant-eating dinosaurs.

▶ **Archelon** had weak jaws and a toothless beak. It may have fed on soft-bodied jellyfish like leatherback turtles do today.

▶ **Placochelys** had a hard toothless beak which it could have used to pluck shellfish off rocks.

▼ **Rutiodon** looks much like a modern crocodile, but it has nostrils between its eyes, not at the tip of the snout.

63

Mammal-like reptiles

The first of the mammal-like reptiles lived more than 300 million years ago. These creatures were the dominant land animals for the next 80 million years, until the dinosaurs began to take over during the Triassic. By the middle of the Jurassic period, the last of the mammal-like reptiles became extinct. However, the most advanced mammal-like reptiles left their mark on the world. They were the direct ancestors of mammals, the animals that dominate life on land today.

Before dinosaurs

Pelycosaurs were mammal-like reptiles which lived before the time of the dinosaurs. These reptiles rapidly evolved from small lizardlike creatures into animals of a much heavier build, with strong jaws and teeth of different shapes.

One interesting pelycosaur was *Dimetrodon*, a reptile with a huge sail-like structure on its back. The framework of the sail was made up of long spines extending from the backbone. In life, a sheet of skin, richly supplied with blood vessels, would have covered the spines. This sail might have been used as a way of controlling body temperature in the same way as the plates on the

▼ **Dimetrodon** was a predatory pelycosaur which lived 30 million years before the dinosaurs.

▲ **Moschops** was a plant-eating mammal-like reptile which lived in the Late Permian, before the time of the dinosaurs. It was about 16 feet long.

◀ **Massetognathus** was a plant-eating cynodont which lived in South America during the Triassic.

backs of stegosaurs (*see pages 56–57*). The pelycosaur might have turned its sail toward the sun to warm itself up, and away from the sun and into the wind to cool down.

More advanced than the pelycosaurs were the therapsids, which were direct ancestors of mammals. The structure of these creatures' skulls allowed for large powerful muscles which made their jaws much more powerful than those of ordinary reptiles. The two most successful groups were the dicynodonts and cynodonts. One of the biggest of the dicynodonts was *Kannemeyeria*, a plant-eating reptile with a huge head. It could have used its hard beak to tear up mouthfuls of leaves and roots which were then ground up by its toothless jaws.

The cynodonts survived the longest of all the mammal-like reptiles. Like the dicynodonts, they had powerfully muscled jaws, but they also had different types of teeth like mammals. The jaws of *Cynognathus*, for example, show that it was a fierce hunter. Its large jaws, which would have had enormous biting power, contained cutting incisor teeth, stabbing canines, and larger cheek teeth for chewing.

▲ **Kannemeyeria** was a bulky dicynodont which measured up to 10 feet long. It lived in the Early Triassic.

▶ **Cynognathus** lived in Africa and South America during the Early Triassic. It was 3 to 4 feet long.

Glossary

Most terms to do with dinosaurs and prehistoric life are explained in the text. So try looking in the index if you cannot find the word you are looking for here.

ammonite   A member of an extinct group of sea-living relatives of today's squid and octopuses. An ammonite had a coiled hard shell inside which lived a soft-bodied animal with tentacles.

amphibian   A four-legged backboned animal that lays its eggs in water. The young pass through a larval (tadpole) stage before becoming adults.

armored dinosaur   An armored dinosaur was covered with plates of bone and bony spikes and knobs which helped to protect it from enemies. There were two kinds of armored dinosaurs—ankylosaurs and nodosaurs. They lived in the Mid Jurassic to Late Cretaceous.

billion   One thousand million.

boneheaded dinosaur   A boneheaded dinosaur had an unusual dome-shaped skull which helped protect its head when it took part in battles with rival male dinosaurs. There were two groups of boneheaded dinosaurs—homalocephalids and pachycephalosaurs.

Carboniferous   The period from 360 to 286 million years ago. The first reptiles lived in the Carboniferous period.

carnivore   An animal that eats the flesh of other animals in order to survive. *Tyrannosaurus* was one of the largest of the carnivorous dinosaurs.

carnosaur   Carnosaurs were the biggest predatory dinosaurs. *Tyrannosaurus* was a carnosaur.

coelurosaur   A coelurosaur was a small, lightly built dinosaur that hunted smaller creatures to eat.

Cretaceous   The period from 135 to 65 million years ago. Dinosaurs were at their most varied in this period but became extinct at its end.

cycad   Cycads were cone-bearing plants which lived before flowering plants. They had stubby trunks and long palmlike leaves.

dromaeosaur   A dromaeosaur was a flesh-eating, fast-running dinosaur.

duckbilled dinosaur   A dinosaur with a long flattened beak. Many duckbills also had strangely shaped crests on their heads.

family   A family is a group of related species. For example, all the species of duckbilled dinosaurs, such as *Lambeosaurus* and *Maiasaura*, belong to the family Hadrosauridae.

fossil   The remains of an animal preserved in rock. Hard body parts, such as teeth and bones, are more likely to form fossils than soft parts. Impressions in rock, such as footprints, can also become fossilized.

geological   A word used to describe things which have to do with the rocks out of which the Earth's crust is built. A geological age is one of the periods of our planet's past, such as the Triassic, Jurassic, and Cretaceous. Each of these lasted many millions of years. The beginning and end of each age is determined by the layers of rocks laid down at those times in the past, and the fossils found in them.

Gondwana   An ancient landmass formed when Pangea broke up about 180 million years ago. Gondwana later split to make the modern continents of South America, Africa, India, Australia, and Antarctica.

herbivore   An animal that eats plants. *Diplodocus* was a herbivorous dinosaur.

horned dinosaur   A horned dinosaur had a large head with long pointed horns and a great sheet of bone called a frill growing out from the back of the skull. This helped protect the dinosaur from attack.

ichthyosaur   A fast-swimming marine reptile, which spent all its life at sea. Ichthyosaurs had sleek, streamlined bodies and lived much like today's dolphins.

iguanodont   An iguanodont was medium to large plant-eating dinosaur. Most iguanodonts had a sharp thumb spike on each hand which they used to defend themselves.

Laurasia   An ancient landmass formed when Pangea broke up about 180 million years ago. Laurasia later split to make the modern continents of North America and Eurasia.

mammal-like reptile   Mammal-like reptiles were the dominant reptiles on Earth before the dinosaurs. The later mammal-like reptiles were the ancestors of the mammals on Earth today.

Mesozoic The era of the Earth's history from 225 to 65 million years ago, which was divided into three periods—the Triassic, Jurassic, and Cretaceous.

order An order is a group of related families. There are two orders of dinosaurs—the Ornithischia (ornithischians) and Saurischia (saurischians). Some large orders are divided into smaller groups called suborders.

Ornithischia One of the two orders into which dinosaurs are divided. The orders differ in the structure of their hip bones. In ornithischian dinosaurs, two of the three hip bones run parallel with one another downward and backward away from the hip joint. All ornithischians fed on plants.

ornithomimid An ornithomimid was a fast-running dinosaur which looked similar to a modern ostrich.

paleontologist A scientist who finds and studies fossils. The fossils can be used to understand what long-extinct creatures looked like and how they lived.

Pangea An ancient continental landmass which formed about 240 million years ago. At this stage of the Earth's history, it seems that all the land was gathered together. Pangea later broke up into two huge landmasses—Laurasia and Gondwana.

plesiosaur A marine reptile with a long neck and flipperlike limbs. Plesiosaurs spent nearly all their lives at sea, but they came to land to lay eggs.

pterosaur A flying reptile which lived at the same time as the dinosaurs. Pterosaurs had wings made of skin attached to an extra-long finger on each hand. There were two kinds of pterosaurs—pterodactyls and rhamphorhynchs.

reptile A four-legged backboned animal that has a dry skin and breathes air. Reptiles lay eggs with tough leathery shells. These hatch into young which look like small versions of their parents.

Saurischia One of the two orders into which dinosaurs are divided. The orders differ in the structure of their hip bones. In saurischian dinosaurs, the three bones of the pelvis connect with one another only near the hip joint where the hind leg meets the hip. Saurischians included both flesh-eating and plant-eating dinosaurs.

sauropod A type of saurischian dinosaur. These long-necked browsing dinosaurs were the largest dinosaurs known and included animals such as *Diplodocus* and *Brachiosaurus*.

scavenger A creature that feeds on the remains of animals that have died naturally or been killed by other flesh eaters.

species A particular type of animal or plant. Members of the same species can mate and produce young.

stegosaur A plant-eating dinosaur with a double row of bony plates along its back. Stegosaurs lived in the Jurassic and Cretaceous periods.

Triassic The period that lasted from 245 to 195 million years ago. The first dinosaurs lived toward the end of this period.

Index

Note: Page numbers in *italic* refer to captions to illustrations

PICTURE ACKNOWLEDGMENTS

l = left; r = right; t = top; c = center; b = bottom

Artwork
All scale diagrams on pp. 39–61 by Mainline Design; 8 Steve Kirk; 9 Mainline Design; 10b Mainline Design; 10t Steve Kirk; 11 Steve Kirk; 12tl Elizabeth Gray; 12r Peter David Scott/Wildlife Art; 13 Elizabeth Gray; 14l Peter David Scott/Wildlife Art; 14r Steve Kirk; 15 Peter David Scott; 16–17 Steve Kirk; 18–19 Peter David Scott/Wildlife Art; 20–21 Peter David Scott/Wildlife Art; 21b Robin Bouttell/Wildlife Art; 22 Mainline Design; 23 Peter David Scott/Wildlife Art; 25 Steve Kirk; 26–27 Mainline Design; 28 Terence Gabbey; 29t Steve Kirk; 30–31 Peter David Scott/Wildlife Art; 33b Gerry Ball/Eikon; 35 Steve Kirk; 36–37 Mainline Design; 38t Elizabeth Gray; 38–39 Peter David Scott/Wildlife Art; 39br Steve Kirk; 40–41 Steve Kirk; 42t Peter David Scott/Wildlife Art; 42b Steve Kirk; 43 Peter David Scott/Wildlife Art; 44–45 Steve Kirk; 46 Peter David Scott/Wildlife Art; 47 Steve Kirk; 48tl Steve Kirk; 48r Peter David Scott/Wildlife Art; 49 Steve Kirk; 50–51 Steve Kirk; 52bl Steve Kirk; 52tr Elizabeth Gray; 53 Steve Kirk; 54t and c Elizabeth Gray; 54b Steve Kirk; 55 Steve Kirk; 56–57 Elizabeth Gray; 57r Steve Kirk; 58–59 Robin Bouttell/Wildlife Art; 60–61 Robin Bouttell/Wildlife Art; 62–63 Steve Kirk; 64–65 Steve Kirk.

Photographs
Endpapers: the Natural History Museum, London; 14 The Natural History Museum, London; 22 Francois Gohier/Ardea; 23 Jim Amos/Science Photo Library; 24 The Natural History Museum, London; 26 Sinclair Stammers/Science Photo Library; 27 The Natural History Museum, London; 31t The Natural History Museum, London; 31b Francois Gohier/Ardea; 32t The Natural History Museum, London; 32bl Peabody Museum of Natural History, Yale University; 32br The Natural History Museum, London; 32–33 J.B. Shackleford/American Museum of Natural History; 33 The Natural History Museum, London; 34–35 The Natural History Museum, London;